An old print showing female snuff-takers.

SNUFF

Ursula Bourne

Shire Publications Ltd

CONTENTS

Printed in Great Britain by C. I. Thomas & Sons (Haverfordwest) Ltd, Press Buildings, Merlins Bridge, Haverfordwest, Dyfed SA61 1XF.

British Library Cataloguing in Publication Data: Bourne, Ursula. Snuff. 1. Snuff. I. Title. 679. 7. ISBN 0-7478-0089-8.

To my daughter Frances and her husband Luis, whose country was amongst the first where snuffing was to be found.

ACKNOWLEDGEMENTS

The author gratefully acknowledges the help she has received from the following: Mr V. S. Rose of G. Smith and Sons, the Snuff Centre; Mr H. E. A. Albin, Secretary of the Society of British Snuff Blenders; Mr M. H. F. Chaytor and staff of Wilsons and Company (Sharrow); Mr G. Forrest and staff of Samuel Gawith and Company, Kendal; Miss R. C. Prentice, Assistant Keeper, Department of Ships and Antiquities, National Maritime Museum, Greenwich; Mr Robert Kleiner, Chinese snuff bottle department, and the staff of the ceramics department of Messrs Sotheby, New Bond Street, London; and her husband, whose advice and interest gave her great encouragement and help.

The publishers acknowledge with gratitude the assistance of Dr D. M. Kalman in the preparation of the book.

Illustrations are acknowledged as follows: Cambridge and County Folk Museum, page 3; Samuel Gawith and Company, pages 12, 14, 15, 23 (top), 28 (bottom); Cadbury Lamb, pages 11 (left and right), 21 (bottom); Jeremy Montagu, page 18; Stephen Moore, page 27 (top left and right); Curator of the Museum of the Marylebone Cricket Club, Lords, page 20 (bottom right); National Railway Museum, York, page 28 (top); Mrs Josephine Pearson, page 20 (top); Mr Rose of G. Smith and Son, pages 1, 5, 6, 8, 17 (left and right), 22, 23 (bottom), 27 (bottom), 30, 31 (left); Sotheby's, pages 19 (left and right), 20 (bottom left), 21 (top), 24, 25; Amoret Tanner, pages 26 (top and bottom), 29 (bottom), 31 (right); Wilsons and Company, pages 9, 10, 13, 16 (bottom), 32.

The cover design is by Rachel Lewis.

A nineteenth-century tobacco sign.

THE HISTORY OF SNUFF

The history of snuff is as fascinating as that of smoking tobacco, for smoking and snuffing have been closely linked through the centuries since tobacco was first discovered by Europeans. Until about 1900 the volume of snuff produced exceeded that of other forms of tobacco, for smoking and chewing.

Contrary to popular belief, it was not Sir Walter Raleigh who introduced tobacco to Europe. A Franciscan friar, Romano Pane, who accompanied Christopher Columbus on his second voyage of discovery to the New World at the end of the fifteenth century, reported on his return that he had seen the inhabitants burning the dried leaves of a certain plant, or 'weed', and inhaling the smoke, or sniffing a powder made from the dried leaves through a Y-shaped cane, the lower end being inserted in the powder and the two upper ends into the nostrils. This plant came to be known as tobacco. Pane stressed that they did this both for enjoyment and for medicinal reasons.

When, in the sixteenth century, the physician and naturalist Fernando Hernandez was sent by Philip II of Spain to Mexico to investigate the natural resources of the country, he brought back with him leaves and seeds of the tobacco plant. This was the first appearance of tobacco in Europe.

Use of the plant spread from Spain to Portugal. In 1560 the French ambassador to Lisbon, Jean Nicot (from whose name the word 'nicotine' is derived), sent some leaves as a gift to the French queen, Catherine de Medici, with instructions on how to use them as snuff to cure her

3

migraine. She may have been the first woman in Europe to take snuff and she became an addict.

At this time tobacco was used in three different ways. In the American colonies the chewing of 'plugs' or ropes of dried and twisted tobacco was favoured. The people of most European countries at first snuffed the powdered leaves, whereas in England at first the leaves were smoked, and snuffing was not adopted until later. For a short while the English were unique in smoking tobacco, for in Ireland and in Scotland the European habit of snuffing was universally adopted.

During the late sixteenth and early seventeenth centuries, in spite of, or possibly because of, the popularity of tobacco both for snuffing and for smoking, opposition to its use began to be heard. Pope Urban VIII, enraged by the habit of some of his clergy of taking snuff, particularly while saying mass, issued an interdict against the use of snuff in places of worship, and this was renewed by his successor. In the reign of Louis XIII of France, his minister Cardinal Richelieu imposed a tax on tobacco — which later helped Louis XIV to finance his military campaigns. In England in 1584 Queen Elizabeth I issued a decree against the 'misuse' of tobacco; and James I not only introduced a tax on tobacco but in 1604 wrote 'A Counterblast to Tobacco', which remains one of the fiercest condemnations of tobacco in all its forms.

During the reign of James I there occurred one of the earliest references to the habit of snuff-taking in England. When the King was to make a visit to the university of Cambridge, the authorities were asked to ban temporarily the use of tobacco, either for smoking or for snuffing, during his stay.

In spite of the tax and royal disapproval, snuff-taking began to take a hold in England. There were two main reasons for this: first, the lower classes had developed the habit of smoking, while the fashionable took snuff in the belief that it was more elegant; and secondly, with the Restoration of Charles II in 1660 many courtiers returned to England from exile in France, where they had adopted the continental habit of snuffing.

In the reign of Queen Anne (1702-14) there was a great rise in the popularity of snuff-taking in England. Many Englishmen returning from the almost continuous Wars of the Spanish Succession on the continent indulged in the habit of snuff-taking, which was now universally popular there; and it was during these years of conflict that an event occurred which made snuff widely and cheaply available to everyone in England, not just the well-to-do. In 1702 Admiral Sir George Rooke's fleet, failing to capture the Spanish port of Cadiz, plundered some smaller ports nearby. These included Port St Mary, where the booty included several thousand barrels and casks of good-quality snuff. On the way home the fleet plundered the port of Vigo, where a number of richly laden Spanish galleons had arrived from Havana, and again the plunder included large quantities of snuff. On return to England the sailors were given the snuff as their share of the booty, and they set about selling it throughout the country, particularly in and around the southern ports. It became popularly known as Vigo Snuff, or Vigo Prize Snuff. It was the first time that large quantities of snuff in its prepared state had arrived in England, and it was sold for about three or four pence a pound. This event gave a great impetus to snuff-taking in England and the habit became as firmly established as it was on the continent; among the upper classes at least, it almost entirely supplanted smoking. When, in 1705, Beau Nash went to Bath and established it as a fashionable resort, he banned smoking in the public rooms; and as Bath became the centre of fashion, London society followed its lead.

The introduction and spread of coffeehouses at the end of the seventeenth century and the beginning of the eighteenth also encouraged the popularity of snuff-taking. There were three thousand coffee-houses in London alone in the eighteenth century. They catered for a broad clientele but, like the clubs which succeeded them, were frequented mostly by men of particular professions or callings. Those around Pall Mall and St James's Street in London attracted the best company, including prominent men of letters. Most, if not all, were snuff-takers, and the taking of snuff was a great feature of the coffee-houses. Such was the ascendancy of snuff-taking over smoking that calling for tobacco or lighting a pipe in a coffee-house was regarded with horror. Of one coffee-house, frequented by fops, a visitor said that the closing of their snuffbox lids made more noise than their tongues.

Notable snuffers of the period included men and women from all walks of life: Alexander Pope, Joseph Addison, Samuel Johnson, Beau Nash, Beau Brummel, Lady Mary Wortley Montagu, David Garrick, Sarah Siddons, Sir Joshua Reynolds, the Duke of Wellington, Lord Nelson, who always took large quantities of snuff with him when he went to sea,

'The French Fireside' by Tomkins, after Ansell: a French lady accepts the offer of a pinch of snuff.

Women had not taken to the habit of smoking but they readily took up snuff-taking. Books on etiquette of the period constantly refer to feminine snuff-taking habits. Ladies were mocked for the popular habit of 'feeding their nostrils with spoons', that is using the tiny snuff-taking spoons which began to be seen. Ladies were also warned that sauce and snuff on the upper lip at dinner was not appealing.

and members of the Royal Family. Queen Anne took snuff, but in moderation. The most hearty snuffer was Queen Charlotte, the wife of George III. Her excessive indulgence in the habit earned her the unattractive soubriquet of 'Snuffy Charlotte', and her family called her 'Old Snuffy'. George himself disliked snuff but he was frequently bullied into taking a pinch just to satisfy his wife.

Queen Charlotte's son, the Prince of Wales, later to become Prince Regent and King George IV, took to the habit with enthusiasm. A prodigious snuffer, he changed his snuff according to the time of the day. One room in each of his palaces was set aside for the storage of snuff, the largest of these being at Windsor. By the time of his death an enormous amount of snuff had been amassed. This was sold, much of it being bought back by his suppliers, Fribourg and Treyer in the Haymarket in London, who in turn resold it, no doubt profitably, under such names as 'The King's Mix', 'The King's Evening Mix' and 'The King's Martinique'.

Some of it was bought by Lord Petersham, perhaps better remembered as the inventor of the Petersham overcoat. He was an eccentric who never went out before the evening and had one snuffbox for every day of the year. He kept 3000-4000 pounds (1400-1800 kg) of snuff in store and had his entire establishment dressed in snuff-coloured livery. The archives of Fribourg and Treyer reveal that for one year Lord Petersham gave up snuffing completely and sold his considerable stocks back to the suppliers. Why he did this is unknown but he did return to the habit with gusto.

Perhaps the unhappiest snuff-taker in history was Mary Lamb, the sister of Charles Lamb. She is now remembered mostly for her rewriting, with her brother, of the *Tales from Shakespeare*. She suffered from insanity, which caused her to kill her own mother. She was left at liberty under the care of her brother and spent her days writing and indulging her passion for snuff-taking. Her consumption of snuff exceeded what she could afford and she resorted to cunning to satisfy her needs. Once a week Miss Lamb did her social rounds, calling throughout the morning on various lady friends for a cup of tea and a chat. She carried in her bag at least a dozen empty snuffboxes. On each call she would take out a box and feign dismay and surprise that it was empty. The hostess would generously insist on filling the box from her own stores. By the end of the morning a good week's supply had been gathered!

Taking a pinch of snuff, a late nineteenth-century drawing by Alfred Concanen (1835-86).

The most remarkable excess by a snuff-taker was committed by Mrs Margaret Thomson, of Boyle Street, Burlington Gardens, Whitechapel, East London, who died on 2nd April 1776. An inveterate and intemperate snuff-taker, Mrs Thomson instructed in her will that her woman servant should line her final resting place with her unwashed handkerchiefs! The coffin containing her body was to be filled with the best Scotch snuff, making it the world's largest snuffbox. She left a sum of money to purchase snuff-coloured beaver hats for her six bearers and stipulated that the men honoured with the job should be the biggest consumers of snuff in the parish. Six maidens accompanied the coffin carrying snuffboxes and the clergyman had to go before them taking copious quantities of snuff. The faithful woman servant followed the cortege placing a liberal handful of snuff each 20 yards (18 metres) in the street for the crowd. As a final act of generosity, two bushels of good-quality snuff were distributed at Mrs Thomson's door on the day of her funeral.

Snuff-taking in the eighteenth and early nineteenth centuries reached proportions which are hardly imaginable today. With royal patronage it became a universal habit, practised by everyone from the lowest in the land to the highest-born aristocrat. The very wealthy and fashionable not only had different boxes and flavoured snuffs for different occasions, but some had a different box for each change of outfit. The fops and beaux vied with one another in matters of snuff etiquette, with complicated and fantastic rituals. One description of the act of taking a pinch, which appeared in every European country in around 1800, divided the ritual into twelve stages:

1. Take the snuffbox with your right hand.
2. Pass the snuffbox to your left hand.
3. Rap the snuffbox.
4. Open the snuffbox.
5. Present the box to the company.
6. Receive it after going the round.
7. Gather up the snuff in the box by striking the side with the middle and fore fingers.
8. Take a pinch of snuff with the right hand.
9. Keep the snuff a moment or two between the fingers before carrying it to the nose.
10. Put the snuff to your nose.
11. Sniff it by precision with both nostrils, and without any grimace.
12. Close the snuffbox with a flourish.

After enjoying its heyday during the reign of George IV snuff began its gradual decline on his death. His successor, William IV, did take snuff, but to a much lesser degree. Queen Victoria, though she appointed royal snuff-makers, did not take snuff herself but only made gifts of it and even this custom soon ceased. During her reign snuff-taking, if not actually frowned upon, came to be regarded with some distaste. One possible reason was that the ritual of snuff-taking had reached such a foppish and ridiculous degree that the sober-minded Victorians began to regard the whole exercise as ludicrous. But snuff continued to enjoy a wide popularity, holding its own against the more expensive and unhealthy smoking of tobacco until the twentieth century. Throughout Victoria's reign, people of all ranks continued to enjoy snuff in amazing quantities, only now the associated glamour had gone. Charles Darwin was a heavy snuff addict in the mid nineteenth century. In an attempt to reduce his intake he kept the snuff container in the hall of his house, so that taking a pinch was an irksome interruption.

A more important cause of the decline of snuff-taking was the introduction of the cigar and the cigar divans. These were tobacco shops, which sold articles for both smoking and snuffing, but they also provided comfortable rooms where customers could converse and smoke — a retreat for many Victorians prohibited from smoking at home. The novels of Charles Dickens reflect the change in attitude to snuff. Many of his characters take snuff but they are invariably either villains, as in *Barnaby Rudge*, or fools as in *Bleak House*.

Women also played a part in the decline of snuffing, for though in earlier years some of the greatest addicts had been women, during the Victorian era the female sex began to regard snuff-taking as demeaning, a habit fit only for the lower classes.

The ledgers of the renowned tobacco and snuff house of Fribourg and Treyer show clearly how snuff-taking declined during the nineteenth century. In 1820 tobacco and cigars represented no more than 10 per cent of sales, and snuff 90 per cent. In 1845 approximately equal amounts were sold, and by 1850 smokers were the greater proportion of customers. In the middle of the century the cigarette made its appearance, its sales being first noted in the Fribourg and Treyer ledgers in 1852. It quickly became extremely popular, partly because it was a novelty, but also because it was more convenient — and more suitable for ladies than either a pipe or a cigar.

However, in spite of competition from the cigarette, the habit of snuff-taking, though it has declined, has by no means disappeared and is thought by many to be increasing again. There are over one million regular snuffers in Britain today, with several thriving manufacturers and blenders producing large quantities of snuff both for the domestic market and for export.

7

A display of snuff by Samuel Gawith of Kendal in various containers.

SNUFF MAKING AND SELLING

Snuff is the most highly processed and expensive of all tobacco products but because tobacco tax is not applied to it in Britain and only small quantities are consumed at a time it is very inexpensive to use. There are two basic processes employed in snuff making. The ancient method of tightly binding rolls of tobacco leaves into 'carottes' and sealing them to ferment in their juices for several years has now mostly been replaced in Britain by quicker methods of saltwater fermentation. Both processes end with the 'cured' or prepared tobacco leaf being pulverised and sieved for uniform quality and texture. For different types of snuff, different parts of the leaf or stem are emphasised.

The types of snuff which are produced are extremely numerous, with variations in size of grain, colour, moisture and flavour. There are well over two hundred produced in Britain and several popular German brands are imported. They can be divided roughly into three groups: those which are moist, dark in colour and coarsely ground: those of medium grain and moisture and medium brown in colour: and the very dry, lightly coloured and finely ground snuffs. All have their devotees and most dedicated snuffers have a variety of snuff in stock to suit

their mood and circumstances. The novice snuffer will probably find the medium snuffs, such as Crumbs of Comfort from Wilsons of Sharrow in Sheffield or Town Clerk from Smith's in London, a good introduction. The heavy moist snuffs and especially the light dry ones are acquired tastes. The fineness of the grain is a matter not of quality but of personal preference.

Within these general categories of dark moist, medium and fine light there exists a wide spectrum of varieties and flavours. These are produced by slight changes in the processing of the tobacco but mostly by the secret blending techniques of each company. Kendal Brown, for example, is one of the oldest snuffs in continual production in England and is still made by Samuel Gawith and Company in Kendal. Kendal Brown is a prime example of the coarse moist dark snuffs. The snuff is produced in a wide selection of flavours by most of the major producers in Britain and is probably something like the 'rappee' snuffs of the past. These coarse snuffs are still popular in the north of England and eastern Scotland. The medium moist snuffs are the most popular and are typified by the 'SP' ranges. The meaning of 'SP' is subject to speculation. In Sheffield it is claimed to stand

8

for 'Sheffield's Pride', but it is most likely to be an early denotation for 'Spanish snuff'. Being mild and moist, the medium range is most adaptable and most popular. This medium type of snuff is prevalent over the south of England. For the snuff experimenter there are unlimited types and combinations in this range, and many flavours and blends go back to Georgian times, if not earlier. The dry fine light snuffs, usually called 'high dry toast', are almost exclusively limited to Celtic tastes. They are popular in Ireland and western Scotland. In the eighteenth century they were also manufactured in Wales. These are a challenge to the beginner's nose and are produced either completely plain or with strong medication added.

The tobacco from which snuff is made is imported from different parts of the world, such as Kentucky, Virginia and North Carolina in the United States, from Brazil, from Malawi and Zimbabwe in Africa and from Madras in India. It arrives in large bales, composed of bundles of dried leaves, known in the trade as 'hands'. Generally the soft parts of the leaves are used for making the darker, moister snuffs, but the midribs and even the stalks are included to make the drier, lighter types. Broken leaves and stalks, known as 'shorts and smalls', which are unsuitable for the manufacture of cigarettes, are also sometimes used, but the quality of the leaf is as high as that used for cigarettes and pipe tobacco.

The nature and quality of the final product depends largely on the choice of leaf and the blending of various types of herbal oils and scents. Manufacturers have their own formulae, which are closely guarded secrets, handed down from generation to generation in what are frequently family firms. In some cases the selected leaf may be damped with salt water and kept at a suitable regulated temperature to induce fermentation, in order to remove impurities which might affect the flavour. The material is then dried in kilns or drying rooms to the extent necessary for the particular kind of snuff being produced.

Most of the snuff imported into England today is made in Bavaria, Germany. There the production still follows the oldest known methods of snuff making. The tobacco is rolled into hard sticks or

Tobacco leaf as imported.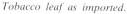

9

Breaking up tobacco leaf.

Hand-testing broken leaf.

'carottes' and sewn up into animal hides, where it ferments naturally. This long process, sometimes taking more than a year, produces a mild Brazilian snuff which is easily consumed in great quantities.

Up to the beginning of the eighteenth century most of the snuff sold in Britain was imported, but with the rising popularity of snuff-taking during that century production in England, Scotland and Ireland, though never rivalling the imported snuff, was considerably increased. Hand grinding, either by simple pestle and mortar or by hand-operated mills similar to coffee mills — a type of which was used by Brazilians in the sixteenth century — was no longer adequate to cope with the demand and power-operated mills were introduced. Early in the century there were some horse-driven mills, but by the middle of the century watermills were adapted to the grinding of snuff. Mills were usually in the countryside, so that snuff-grinding was very much a rural industry. This may seem to be contradicted by the location of the mill of one of the largest producers today, Wilsons of Sharrow, in the heart of a busy shopping district of Sheffield. Tucked away behind a supermarket are a fine Georgian building and others of earlier date, facing a large millpond, with ducks and moorhens nesting on the tree-lined banks. An enormous waterwheel still powers some of the machinery as it has done for over two hundred years, though steam power was introduced in 1797. The mill has

Left: 'De Ster' wind-powered snuff mill at Rotterdam in Holland.

Right: Inside 'De Ster' mill at Rotterdam. In these barrels the tobacco is cut up by blades before being ground.

been owned by the Wilson family since 1737. In the 1740s Joseph Wilson, a silversmith who made Sheffield plate, started making snuff, and the business has been carried on by the family ever since. Snuff is made in a great variety of flavours and much of it is exported.

The mill of another important present-day snuff-maker, Samuel Gawith and Company, is also now situated in a town, Kendal. But it was in the Lakeland countryside, at a watermill, that Thomas Harrison, who had learned snuff making in Scotland, started making the original Kendal Brown snuff in 1792 and it was only in 1920 that production was concentrated at the mill in Kendal, though some of the machinery installed there is said to be the oldest working mechanism in Britain. Like Wilsons of Sharrow and other snuff manufacturers, the firm is a

family one. The original Samuel Gawith was a son-in-law of Thomas Harrison, and he was succeeded by several generations of Gawiths. Much of the snuff produced is sold in Britain, particularly in Birmingham, where there is a large Asian population, many of whom have a habit of taking snuff. Besides the many usual varieties, the firm will make up a snuff to suit the requirement of an individual customer.

Although there have been snuff factories in the south of England — a mill at Mitcham in Surrey supplied much of the English snuff sold in London until snuff making was replaced by lavender growing, and a factory at Devizes in Wiltshire was operating until 1963 — most production is now in the north of England, especially around Sheffield and Kendal. As well as Samuel Gawith and Company,

Workers and machinery, Samuel Gawith's mill, Kendal, about 1930.

A water-powered grinding mill of about 1740, at Wilsons of Sharrow, Sheffield.

Tobacco-grinding machinery.

Gawith Hoggarth and Company also have their mill at Kendal. The reason for this concentration of production in these areas may have been the greater availability of water power.

In these mills most of the older grinders are simply power-driven pestles and mortars, with an iron pestle rotating in an oak-lined mortar, though roller-grinders were used in some mills. Later machines have rotating steel pestles revolving in steel mortars, the powder being collected from the edges. There are sometimes separate machines for producing the different grains of powder required, or the material may be ground several times to produce the desired fineness. After grinding, the powder is sieved to obtain an even texture, silk sieves being used for the finest.

After the crude work of grinding and sieving the snuff is completed, it is usually aged in oak barrels like a fine wine to develop the nose or bouquet. The aging may take from a few months to over a year to complete. Then the snuff is either marketed plain or blended and flavoured. The methods and variations of making the individual types of snuff are too numerous to describe in detail. Basically the ground snuff is scented delicately or strongly with pure herbal essential oils. In Great Britain the use of synthetic oils is forbidden. The most popular oils are bergamot, peppermint, violet, attar of roses and spearmint. Snuff cocktails are then produced by blending these snuffs into new combinations. The individual can satisfy the nose with unending mixtures of snuff. Also very popular are the medicated snuffs, heavily laced with menthol and oil of eucalyptus. These are of great use in relieving catarrh and hay fever and in reducing cold symptoms. The wide difference in the colour of snuff is due entirely to the type of leaf used, as nothing artificial is allowed in the blend.

The names of some of the hundreds of varieties of snuff on sale indicate simply the scent or flavour, such as Peppermint, Attar of Roses, Wallflower, Garden Mint and Golden Lavender. Others are named after the people for whom they were originally made or with whom they were favourites, such as Town Clerk, James Robertson Justice and Prince's Dark (for the Prince Regent), or after their place of origin, such as Best Brazil, Cuba, Masulipatam and Kendal Brown.

Some blends are known merely as numbers, such as Number 74, which refers to 74 Charing Cross Road, the location of Smith and Sons, the famous London snuff specialist. Many of the exotic names such as Vanity Fair and Grand Opera have unusual scents which somehow reflect the names they bear. Some names are of great age, such as Crumbs of Comfort, which is said to be associated with Queen Charlotte. One of the most expensive snuffs, Café Royale, is a blend of North American and oriental tobaccos, specially treated and perfumed with essential oil of coffee and certain spices, and is kept in sealed bottles for a year before being sold.

During the great period of snuff-taking the most notable retailer of snuff and tobacco in London was the firm of Fribourg and Treyer. This was established in 1751 by a Swiss, Peter Fribourg, in a handsome building at number 34 in the Haymarket. The business has now been closed, but the building, with steps leading up to the door between a pair of bow windows, has been preserved. During the eighteenth century the Haymarket became one of the most fashionable parts of London, and the clientele of Fribourg and Treyer included most of the notable personalities of the time, including royalty. The ledgers of the firm have been preserved since 1764 and are a valuable source of information about its customers, the quantities and sorts of snuff and tobacco sold, and the prices. From

them we learn that the price of snuff was generally four or five shillings a pound (0.45 kg), or possibly six shillings for some special sorts. At the beginning of the eighteenth century Vigo Snuff was sold for about four or five pence a pound. The quantities sold seem very large, an order for 6 pounds (2.7 kg) not being unusual. Though most of the snuff sold was imported from France, Germany, Holland, Spain and Brazil, and included very little Irish or Scotch, the export book shows that between 1800 and 1811 snuff was exported to many parts of the world, such as Madeira, the East and West Indies and Calcutta, and even to Lisbon and Frankfurt, which were themselves producers of high-quality snuffs.

Another notable snuff shop in London, which still remains, is that of G. Smith and Sons, the Snuff Centre, at number 74 Charing Cross Road. The firm, established in 1869, had previously been in Covent Garden but moved in 1886 to Charing Cross Road, where it was the first shop to be opened. The building is small and might easily be overlooked, between its larger neighbours; the office at the back of the shop is also small and

A display at Samuel Gawith, Kendal, showing types of tobacco leaf.

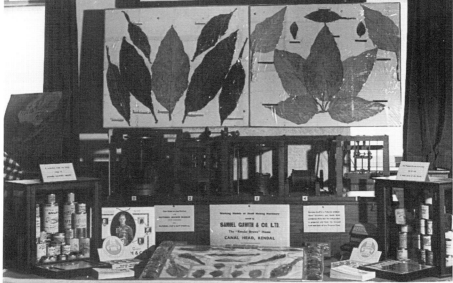

Above: *The snuff and tobacco shop of Fribourg and Treyer was established in Haymarket, London, in 1751.*

Right: *The figure of a Highland snuff-taker at the entrance to Wilsons' mill at Sharrow.*

has a Victorian air. Yet business is brisk, with exports to private customers all over the world, and agents in many countries, including the United States, Canada, Japan, West Africa and Saudi Arabia. Smith's are now handling the range of snuffs made famous by the defunct Fribourg and Treyer.

The shop window of Smith and Sons is a delight for the snuff-taker. There can be seen a wide range of snuffboxes in pewter, wood and horn. Tucked away amongst the types of snuff on display, one can see tiny snuff spoons and enormous ram's horn mulls. Dominating the window is the statue of a kilted Highlander.

The kilted Highland figure has a strong

16

The Snuff Centre (G. Smith and Sons), Charing Cross Road, London. (Left) Weighing snuff and (right) the exterior of the shop.

connection with snuff, for as a sign outside premises it denotes that snuff can be purchased within. A number of these handsome figures can still be found, though they are becoming rarer. They are frequently made of wood and painted, some of them being almost life-sized. The reason for the Highlander being a symbol of snuff is obscure, but it may be a reflection of the great popularity of snuff among the ordinary folk of the Scottish Highlands. Boswell recounts an incident on his journey to the High-

lands with Dr Johnson in 1773 when in return for the hospitality of an old peasant woman they gave her a shilling 'and she begged snuff, for snuff is the luxury of these Highland cottagers'.

From time to time statues of black slaves were used as signs for snuff shops, the connection between tobacco and slavery being obvious. Wooden likenesses of Napoleon, history's most famous snuffer, formerly rivalled the Highlander and can still be seen outside several provincial tobacconists.

An eighteenth- or nineteenth-century Chinese snuff bottle of rock crystal (back), painted internally, with an agate stopper; (second row) modern pewter boxes; (third row, from left to right) an English pinchbeck and agate box, probably early nineteenth-century, and a silver stopper and spoon of the late nineteenth or early twentieth century with a Chinese jade snuff bottle; (front) silver boxes from Birmingham, dated (left to right) 1967, 1807 and 1816.

SNUFF ACCESSORIES

The most important item of equipment for the snuff-taker is something in which to carry the snuff — a snuffbox. This might be said to be indispensable, except that some people have tried to do without one. Dr Johnson, saying that he could not afford a snuffbox, carried his snuff in a pocket of his waistcoat. However, this was not entirely satisfactory, for it was said that considerable quantities ended up on his waistcoat or on the floor. Napoleon I, who took more than 7 pounds (3 kg) of snuff per month, is also said to have carried the snuff loose in his waistcoat pockets, but he is also said to

have left behind a collection of hundreds of boxes.

Not all owners of snuffboxes take snuff, however. Indeed there have been some who abhorred the habit. The French king Louis XIII and his minister, Cardinal Richelieu, had fine collections, although they were opposed to the use of tobacco in any form. Today, when the value of antiques and works of art is so great that they are regarded as a form of investment, snuffboxes, as collector's pieces, fetch high prices.

Snuffboxes range from simple serviceable ones, often wooden, to those made

18

Left: *A Meissen painted and gold-mounted snuffbox, 1740.*

Right: *A Meissen silver-gilt snuffbox, c.1760, with a portrait of Elizabeth of Russia inside the lid. The outside was decorated in the nineteenth century with pictures of soldiers in an encampment.*

of gold or silver, intricately decorated and even jewelled. Other materials used include ivory, jade, amber, enamel and porcelain. Today most good snuff dealers will have a range of usable snuffboxes and bottles. Wood, pewter and horn make the most serviceable boxes, but they are never completely air-tight, and so the snuff-taker is recommended not to keep more than one or two days' supply in his box. The serious user of snuff stores the snuff in sealed bottles or jars.

An essential requisite of a snuffbox is that the lid should fit tightly, as snuff is sensitive to moisture and contamination. The earliest boxes were made of wood and it was found impossible, at first, to make them air-tight, as the hinge of the lid had to be fitted, whereas in metal boxes the rollers of the hinge could be formed as parts of the lid and of the box. This difficulty was finally overcome, at

the end of the eighteenth century, by a Scot, James Sandy. A cripple, he was confined to his bed, which he had designed to serve also as a workshop, and in which he carried on his work in wood and metal. He made several inventions, one of which was an air-tight hinge for a wooden snuffbox. This consisted of a fine brass rod encased in seven tightly fitting rollers, four being fashioned from the back of the box and three from the edge of the lid, turning on the rod. The hinge works like the old-fashioned bolt of a door. Called Laurencekirk boxes, from the village in which Sandy lived, his snuffboxes became widely known and copied, the hinge being used on well made boxes through the Edwardian era.

In spite of the initial difficulty of making a wooden box air-tight, wood was at first the most commonly used material. It has always been plentiful, and even the poorest snuffer could make a rough

19

and simple box. Many kinds of wood have been used, from pine to mahogany and ebony. A snuffbox presented to George IV when he visited Scotland was made from the woods of trees immortalised in Scottish songs and ballads. Not only were snuffboxes made from a variety of kinds of wood, but in some cases the wood itself was significant. Some were made from a mulberry tree which grew in Shakespeare's garden in Stratford-upon-Avon, others from the wooden decks of HMS *Victory* and even the table upon which Wellington wrote his despatch at Waterloo. Wood being ideal for carving, some ornate and unusually shaped boxes were made.

Both gold and silver have been used in the making of snuffboxes. They are suitable for engraving and embossing. On some boxes the design was impressed inwards on the lid; on others it was pressed outwards, giving a raised pattern. More elaborate boxes combined gold or silver with other materials, such as porcelain, mother-of-pearl and tortoiseshell;

An ebony snuffbox in the form of a shoe.

others were embellished with jewels, a large jewel sometimes being the point of pressure to open the box.

Although gold snuffboxes were made in both England and France, by far the greater number came from France. These are remarkable for their lavish and ornate decoration, whereas the English boxes, though often beautifully engraved, are more solid in appearance.

Silver snuffboxes also were made in both countries, as well as elsewhere, those bearing English, Irish and Scottish hallmarks being the most numerous and some of the finest.

Left: *A Meissen gold-mounted snuffbox of 1750, the inside of the lid painted with a scene of elegant ladies and gentlemen watching a comet.*

Right: *A mother-of-pearl and silver-gilt snuffbox, presented for the use of members of the Marylebone Cricket Club in the Club Room by Benjamin Aislebie, Secretary 1822-42.*

A rectangular Birmingham snuffbox (top left), c.1755, gilt metal mount, lid with a picture of a fortune-teller. (Below) Circular Birmingham snuffbox, c.1755, metal-mounted, painted with a quayside scene. (Top right) Rare commemorative snuffbox of 1760, printed with a scene of young George III. flanked by Father Time, comforting a weeping Britannia at a tomb bearing a profile of George II and the inscription 'George II — Glorious'.

Some of the most beautiful boxes are those made of enamel or porcelain, for these two materials are particularly suitable for painting and a number of artists used their talents in this field. In England one of the best known was the miniaturist and Royal Academician Richard Cosway. He was later appointed to the household of the Prince Regent, and his boxes have become valuable collector's pieces.

Papier-mâché boxes are in many ways ideal. They do not need lining, as do those of wood and some other materials;

Victorian papier-mâché snuffbox decorated with a paper print of Gloucester Old Spot pigs.

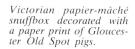

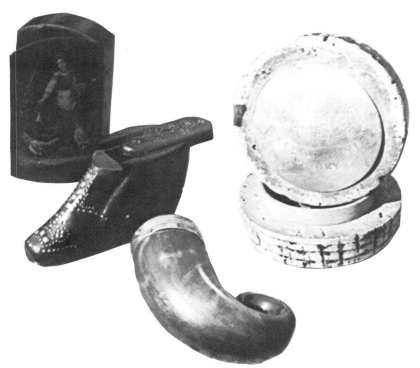

Snuff containers: a painted wooden box, a box in the form of a boot, a horn and a circular cork box.

unlike metal boxes they keep the snuff at an equable temperature, and the surface is admirable for lacquer or painting. Their only failing is the hinge, which, instead of the inconspicuous Laurencekirk hinge of the wooden box, is an exposed one of brass, liable to clogging with snuff.

Horn was, with wood, one of the materials from which early snuffboxes were made. The horns of rams, goats and cattle were also used in the making of the large snuff containers known as mulls. The snuff was contained in the wide end, which was closed by a stopper or lid, often decorated in silver. Most are too large for the pocket, but the smaller ones could be worn on a belt. The larger ones, sometimes comprising a whole ram's head, stand on a table and are used as communal snuffboxes. They are found in a number of regimental messes, particularly in Scotland, where they originated. Some carry small implements such as a rasp, a rake for breaking up lumps in the snuff and a hare's foot for removing surplus powder.

There are communal snuffboxes other than those made of horn. One of the most famous is that in the House of Commons. It is not known when the House first had a common box, but the Georgian silver one in use at the time of the Second World War was destroyed in the Blitz. The present box, in the charge of the Chief Doorkeeper, is a simple wooden one, divided into two compartments lined with pewter, and bearing a silver plate on the lid with a list of doorkeepers. It is, however, historic as the wood from which it was made came from timbers from the damaged House.

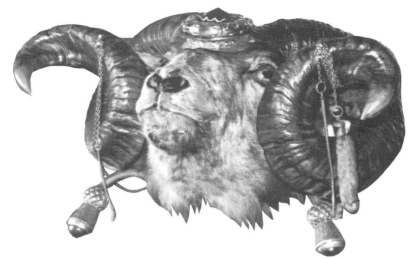

A ram's head mull, hung with a silver spoon and rake and a hare's foot.
A fine example of a ram's head mull with a decorated silver lid.

Chinese glass and crystal snuff bottles, the insides painted.

An altogether different snuff container is the snuff bottle. These are a speciality of the Chinese, and some exquisite examples have been made in that country, particularly during the Ming period of the seventeenth century. They are usually small, about 3 inches (75 mm) high, and are made of a number of materials besides glass, including porcelain, jade and ivory. Those of glass are painted on the inside, the artist lying on his back so that he could work through the narrow neck of the bottle. The snuff was extracted with a small spoon, often attached to the

24

Chinese snuff bottles, porcelain and glass overlay.

stopper of the bottle. Although such spoons were first made in China, they later became popular in Europe, especially among fastidious women. In Victorian times there were cut glass snuff bottles, very much like scent bottles, with brass spoons attached to their ground glass stoppers, although they were rare.

Much of today's snuff is machine-ground, but during the seventeenth and eighteenth centuries many snuff-takers grated their own. The dried tobacco leaf was tightly rolled into what is known as

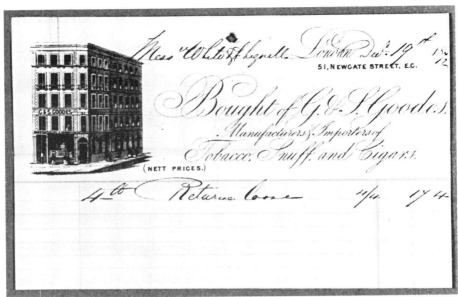

A billhead of G. and S. Goodes, manufacturers and importers of snuff, tobacco and cigars, dated 1872, illustrating the company's premises at 51, Newgate, London EC.

A billhead of Jeconiah Ashley of the Strand, London, dated 21st September 1737. It is the receipt for £3 10s paid for 'a neat snuffbox'.

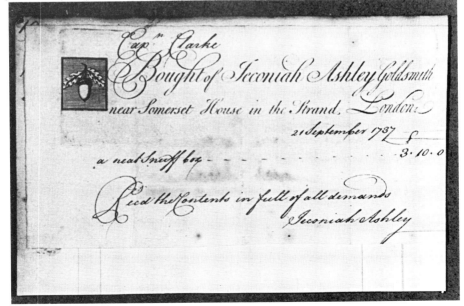

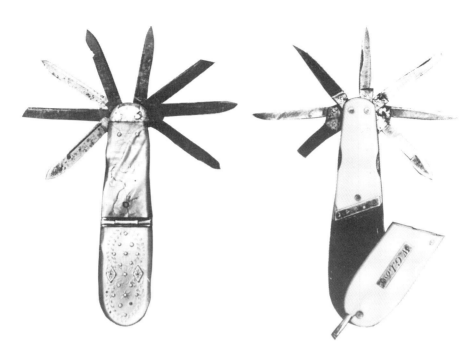

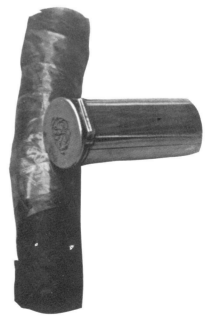

Above, left and right: *Two examples of a combined snuffbox and penknife.*

Right: *A pocket snuff rasp, with a 'carotte' of tobacco.*

a 'carotte', from the French word for a carrot, referring to its shape, and rasps were used to grate these in much the same way as nutmeg is grated on a nutmeg grater. These rasps were made in the shape of elongated boxes, generally tapering, 4 or 5 inches (100-25 mm) long, which easily fitted into the pocket. The top was flat, in the form of a grater, and the bottom concave, forming a cavity into which the grated snuff fell. Rasps were sometimes incorporated in snuffboxes, and examples of these can be seen in snuffbox collections, such as the one in the Victoria and Albert Museum. In Iceland, whose tiny population contains a high percentage of snuffers, there are still a few sheep farmers who grate their own fresh snuff by the 'carotte' method.

27

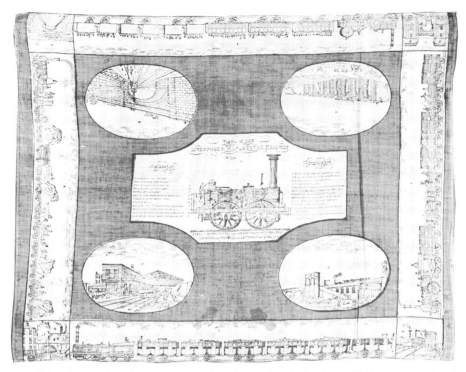

A snuff handkerchief depicting scenes on the Liverpool and Manchester Railway, issued for the opening of the line on 15th September 1830, with explanations in English and French. This has been reproduced as a headsquare for the National Railway Museum, York.

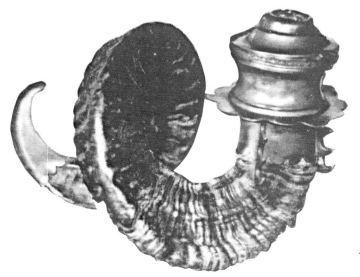

A single-horn mull.

Above: On the upper shelf, various snuffboxes; on the lower shelf, a picture of a monk taking snuff, a 'Toby' taking snuff and other objects standing on a polkadot snuff handkerchief.

Left: A tobacconist's triangular paper envelope for snuff.

WILSONS & CO.
CELEBRATED
SHARROW MILLS
SNUFF
SHEFFIELD.

In the seventeenth and eighteenth centuries fashion required that, after snuffing, one hand and the upper lip should be dusted with a special snuff handkerchief. These were first made of lawn, often edged with fine lace. Later they were made of cambric or cotton and became known as snuff napkins. Silk also was used, the earliest examples appearing in 1721. In order to hide snuff stains these handkerchiefs were usually dyed snuff brown, but later they were colour-printed. Today snuff handkerchiefs can be bought in bright colours, particularly red with white polkadot designs. Brown snuff handkerchiefs are still to be seen plentifully in northern markets such as Chesterfield.

A customer samples some snuff offered to both nostrils.

WHY TAKE SNUFF?

In spite of competition from cigarettes, cigars and pipes, there are still many people who take snuff today. Since the habit, unlike smoking, is a private one there are, no doubt, many takers of snuff whose habit is unknown to all but their closest acquaintances.

There have always been certain trades and professions in which snuff-taking is popular, particularly those in which smoking is forbidden. Workers in printing and tailoring, for example, have taken snuff almost since it was introduced. Snuff-taking has been popular with coal miners, as there is no risk of setting off an explosion. Miners sometimes hold competitions to see who can snuff up a long line of snuff from the handle of a shovel or pickaxe.

Each year in England there are regional snuff-taking competitions organised by the British snuff clubs. These remarkable events have championships both for men and for women. Usually twenty or so contestants sit along a table and are each given a snuff spoon of a uniform snuff on the backs of the hands. They are judged on their neatness of capacity. The money raised by the competition usually goes to local charities.

In courts of law and in both Houses of Parliament, where smoking is forbidden, snuff-taking is indulged in. The taking of snuff has a stimulating effect, and it is said that many lawyers, when confronted by an awkward point or question, take a pinch of snuff, not only to clear the brain but also to give time for consideration. Ministers of religion are also known to indulge in the habit, when it would be unseemly to smoke a pipe or cigarette.

As an aid to clearing the mind, quite a number of motorists and lorry drivers, particularly those undertaking long journeys, find a pinch of snuff invigorating

Left: *A clerical snuff-taker.*

Right: *A German postcard of c.1908 showing a man taking a pinch of snuff from his snuffbox.*

and invaluable in keeping their senses alert. Many people suffering from a heavy cold have found that taking a pinch of snuff brings relief and clears the head. Snuff-takers also seem to be less prone to colds in the head and similar complaints, such as catarrh.

British medical doctors, according to reports in both the *Lancet* and the *British Medical Journal*, have carried out extensive trials on snuff-takers. They have also examined the medical records of snuff users both past and present and they conclude that taking snuff is at worst a harmless habit. This is reflected in the fact that all tobacco tax has been removed from snuff and it is not required to carry any health warnings. The snuffer does receive a hefty dose of nicotine and Dr Russell has written in the *Lancet* that it is likely that snuff would be useful to help smokers break their dangerous habit.

When compared to smoking with its personal health risk and fire hazard, and the extreme unpleasantness it causes the passive smoker, it is apparent that a new age of snuff is well overdue.

The buildings of Wilsons' mill at Sharrow, Sheffield.

FURTHER READING

Arlott, John. *The Snuff Shop*. Michael Joseph, 1974.
McCausland, Hugh. *Snuff and Snuff Boxes*. Batchworth Press, 1951.
Shepherd, C. W. *Snuff Yesterday and Today*. G. Smith and Sons, London, 1963.

MUSEUM OF SNUFF
Schnupftabakmuseum, Spitalstrasse, Grafenau, Bavaria, Germany.